RUGBY FOR HEROES

SKILLS & TECHNIQUES

Illustrated by

Paul Trevillion

Written by Norman Harris

BUCKLEY-BENNION (PUBLISHING) LIMITED

RUGBY FOR HEROES

SKILLS & TECHNIQUES

ACKNOWLEDGEMENT

Working on this book has given great pleasure to many. Paul Trevillion has the temperament as well as the talent of a true artist - dull he is not - whilst Norman Harris has the eye of an eagle and a talon sharp way with words. The Leicester Tigers have been great fun to work with but then so too have our sponsors NEXT and VULKAN.

Our hope is that the enjoyment we have all had in putting this book together will shine through and rub off on you as you read on.

This book is dedicated to the new era of rugby and all aspiring heroes.

E.B.

'Hands on' by author & illustrator

- *Published by Buckley-Bennion (Publishing) Limited*
  The Beeches, 42 West Street, Godmanchester,
  Huntingdon, Cambs PE18 8HH
  Telephone: 01480 414040 Facsimile: 01480 414441

- *Edited by Emrys Bowen*
- *Designed by David G. Cook*
- *Photography: Andrew Maw*
  Jon Murrell
  Associated Sports Photography, Leicester
- *Reproduction by Gildenburg Reprographics, Peterborough.*
- *Printed in England by BPC*

ISBN: 1 901575 00 4

CONTENTS

FOREWORD

As England hooker, Peter Wheeler won 42 caps between 1975 and 1984, captained England when they beat the All Blacks at Twickenham in 1983, and went on three Lions tours. He is now chief executive of the Leicester club.

BY PETER WHEELER

EVERY MAN A LION

The greatest memories of my own rugby career are associated with being on tour with the British Lions. And when I think what life must be like for today's leading club players I can only imagine that it must be like being on tour with the Lions ... all the time.

Representing the Lions on foreign soil fills you with immense pride, and a desire to play with EXCELLENCE. That seems true, too, of today's professional club rugby. The players dedicate themselves not only to playing winning rugby, but also to being the very best they can be.

Today's player gets dietary advice, he is taught how to apply himself mentally, and above all he gets a lot of help in analysing the technical requirements of his position - be it prop, flanker or fullback. This is the big contrast with rugby of even five or six years ago. The difference isn't so much in the amount of training done, but in the way coaching is now focused so sharply. In my day, we just did more running if we wanted to be fitter, there was a lot of scrummage and lineout work, and training was very repetitive. Now we see imaginative drills being constructed to hone the most particular skills - some of which may be required only once or twice in a game, though at moments when they're critical.

Ideas are borrowed, too, from other sports. Cast your eye on the ball skills routines later in this book. If they make you think of basketball, that doesn't mean we're abandoning the scrum and lineout cornerstones of rugby union, No, it means we want rugby to be a game of strength and speed and skill. We want the best of everything that our game can offer. And this exciting season - with some vivid European Cup contests producing a step up in quality - has shown us that we don't yet know the limit of our game's appeal.

Certainly, rugby is a game for heroes. I enthusiastically welcome this book.

INTRODUCTION

BY BOB DWYER

PERFECT MEANS PERFECT

Every coach has a vision of his 'ideal' rugby. My ideal can be described in two words: precision technique. It's an ideal to which any player can aspire, and the techniques illustrated so thoughtfully and clearly - and presented so vividly - in this book apply equally to players on the verge of national selection and to those aspiring to the school First Fifteen.

Bob Dwyer coached Australia from 1982-83 and 1988-95, including victory in the 1991 World Cup, and subsequently Racing Club de France and Leicester.

I always say to players: "Practice doesn't make perfect, only *perfect* practice makes perfect".

Perfect practice means the application of correct technique - first time, every time - so that subsequently, under pressure, your technique holds up. It's interesting that slow motion video of good players always reveals perfect technique.

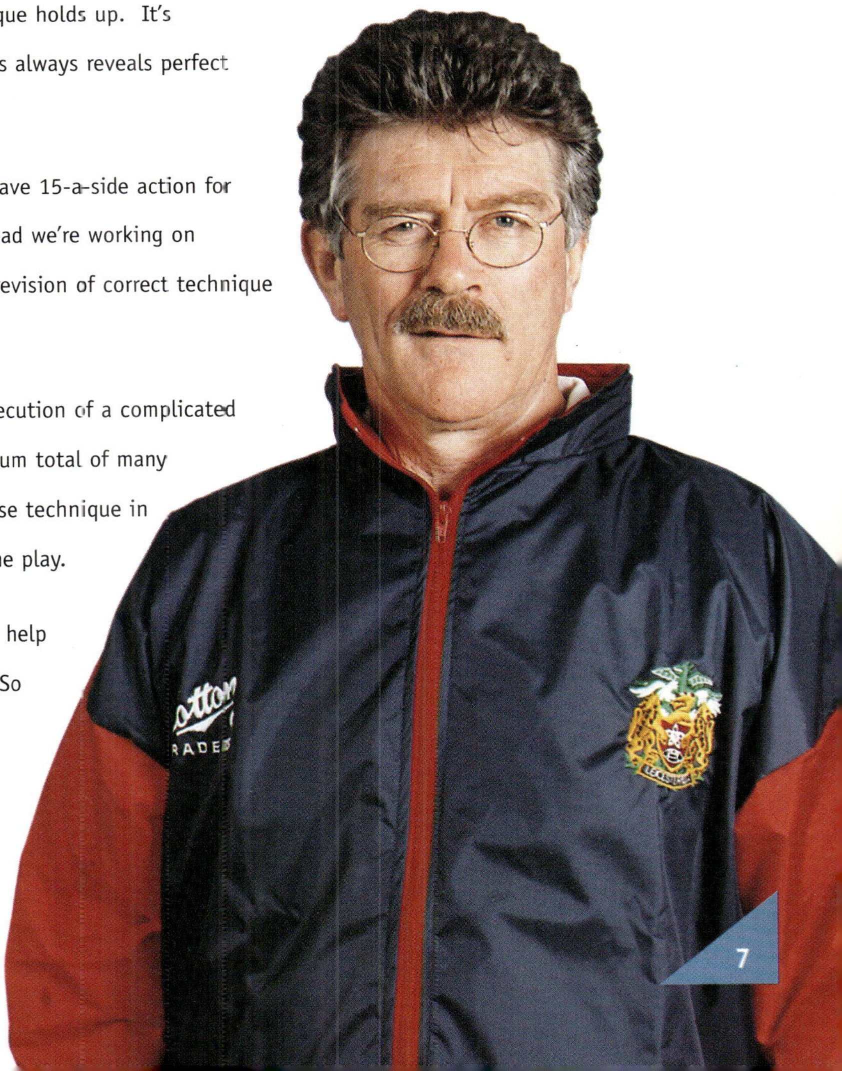

In a two hour Leicester training session we will have 15-a-side action for only 20 minutes, and sometimes not at all. Instead we're working on individual practice - the constant repetition and revision of correct technique in every area.

What appears on the surface to be a precision execution of a complicated backline play will be seen on analysis to be the sum total of many simple actions. And it is the application of precise technique in each of these actions which will make or break the play.

There is a real need for technical advice that will help young players to put their skills to good effect. So I too enthusiastically welcome this book. It is all about excellence.

Mizuno
Mizuno

The Ten Basic Positions

FULLBACK

Once, a fullback was judged purely on his defensive abilities - like a football goalkeeper. Now, he is rated above all for his attacking ability. He has a unique chance to attack because he's the only player who isn't marked by the opposition. He, almost alone, has the exciting opportunity to break through a line of players and run free in space. He should be always looking to enter the line - even if only as a decoy - and on different angles. As an extra winger, he must have real speed, and do the same sort of sprint work as a winger.

THE EXTRA ATTACKER

With the chance to turn defence into attack he can totally change the game, but he can also badly damage the morale of his side if he lets his teammates down on the basics. He has to be brave and confident in the catching of high kicks, ultra reliable in his line kicking. So, he has to be brilliant, and also Mr Reliable. It's a tough combination.

WORLD'S BEST

ANDRE JOUBERT

South Africa

A well proportioned physique, and a balanced running action, means that Joubert is both faster and stronger than he may look. There isn't a better defensive fullback in the world game and few more dangerous attackers.

FULLBACK

special practice

❶

❷

The almost unique test that the fullback must pass is the high ball. So his special practice is to take such kicks with attackers bearing down on him - and with a defender ready to assist.

He has to learn not to glance at the attackers, and to time his jump so that the top of it coincides with the ball's arrival. And he must be turning in the air so that when he takes the ball he is side-on. This means that if he loses the ball it is less likely to be a knock-on - and also that he can protect it instantly, with the help of supporting players.

4

3

WING

No other player in rugby is *expected* to score when he gets half a chance, and no other is judged on what may well be just two or three such chances in a game. For the winger, as often as not, these chances will come in the corner. Getting the ball down before a flying defender knocks him - and the corner flag - into touch requires, above all, extreme self-belief. Those who keep winning in these millisecond brushes with the corner flag clearly establish themselves as the best, like Rory Underwood and Ieuan Evans.

WORLD'S BEST

JONAH LOMU

New Zealand

A giant-like 19 stones, and with a 100m time of 10.8, Lomu tends to go through defenders like a high speed tank. His four tries destroyed England in the 1995 World Cup Final, and made him rugby's most talked about player.

THE CORNER MAN

They believe that they WILL come out best, that they WON'T be tackled into touch, that they WILL be strong enough to fight their way back infield. A change of pace, too, is a key requirement. In the classic move the winger 'fixes' his opposite number by making him slow down or stop, then hits the accelerator to burn past him on the outside. A lot of practice can hone these skills, making the beating of a single opponent almost instinctive - and building the confidence, even arrogance, that marks a true ace.

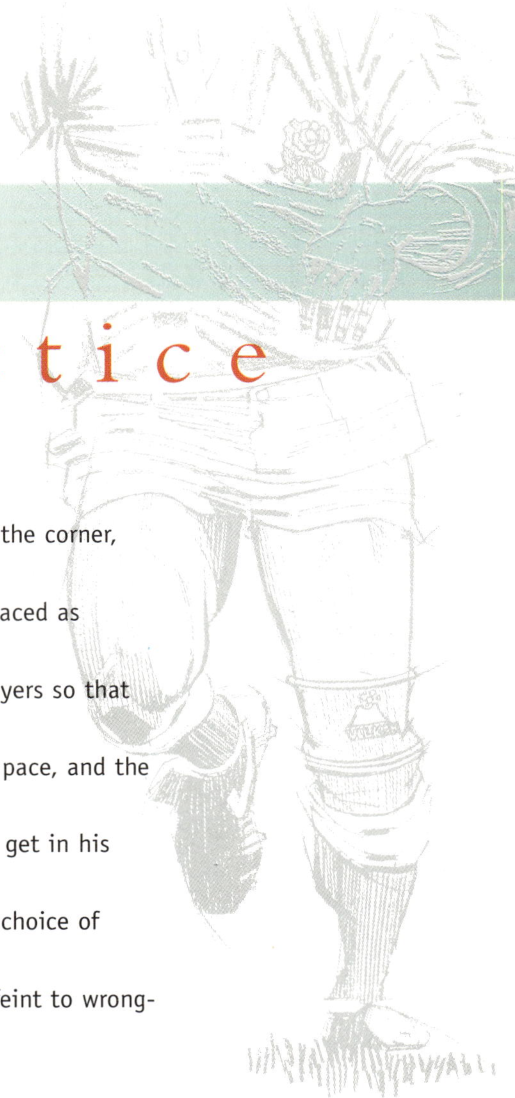

Wing

special practice

With the ball, the winger starts running for the corner, with only one defender (ideally, a fullback) placed as shown. Position both players so that the winger can reach top pace, and the defender just has time to get in his way. The winger has the choice of swerving in or out - probably with an initial feint to wrong-foot the defender.

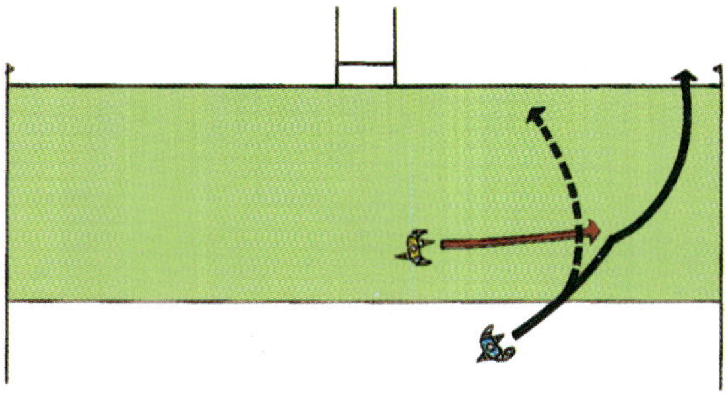

The exercise is made more challenging by the addition of a second defender arriving a little deeper in the 22. The winger has to repeat his swerve routine, though he is now on a different line. Simple exercises like this will quickly build confidence and judgement, and lead to the instinctive beating of a single opponent in a match situation.

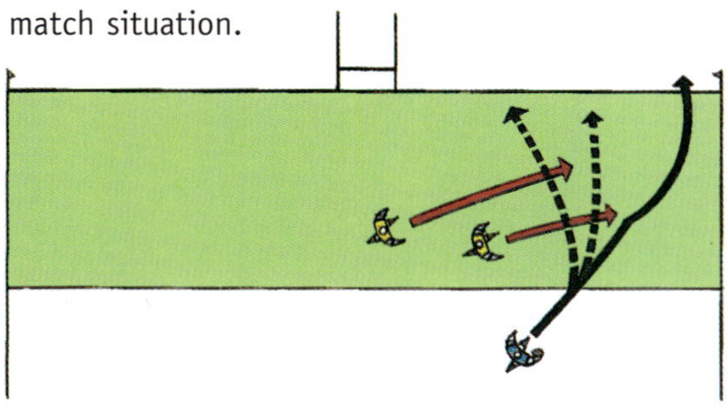

IRFU

CENTRE

THE PASS GIVER

Every back has to be able to pass, but this is the SPECIAL skill of the centre. Not often will he be able to beat his opposite number in a straight one-to-one, but his pass may release someone coming at speed on either side. The inside centre tends to be the stronger player, probably shorter striding with strong thighs that give him the chance to drive a few yards through the tackle (the Will Carling type) while the outside centre will be longer striding and a little faster, with a good outside swerve (the Jeremy Guscott type).

The centres MUST run straight if they are to open up space. And their nerve has to be strong. At the highest level, passes have to be coolly given and taken in the face of fast-moving defenders intent on landing crunching tackles - and made with relaxed hands, and not 'fired' at the receiver. There are plenty of good centres who tackle hard. But only a few catch the eye for cool, accurate passing under pressure. These are the CREATORS.

WORLD'S BEST

JEREMY GUSCOTT

England

With Rory Underwood, England's classiest player of the 1990s. His acceleration brings in mind a stretch limousine, puzzling defenders as he glides rather than explodes, away from them. It is a gift which sets him apart, even among international centres.

Two centres, plus wing, run the ball at speed at two defenders. Both centres must commit the defender before passing. They must learn to do this coolly, with the opponents 'in their face' and ready to tackle. In this three-against-two situation the winger should always be set free. There should be no chance of either defender making ground to make a covering tackle.

CENTRE
special practice

1

2

3

4

FLY-HALF

Not long ago, many fly-halves were nuggety types who kept belting the ball high in the air or running at the opposition with the help of their back-row forwards. But the modern fly-half is a true pivot. He puts himself under pressure, for the benefit of those outside him. Standing teasingly close to the would-be tacklers, he draws their fire before moving the ball somewhere else.

WORLD'S BEST

ANDREW MEHRTENS

New Zealand

An expert distributor of the ball, Mehrtens was just what the ambitious All Blacks wanted when Grant Fox's reign ended. He reached 100 international points in world record time, doing it in only his fifth match - the dramatic 1995 World Cup semi-final against England.

Watch New Zealand's Andrew Mehrtens. Receiving a relatively short pass, he's barely moving as he gets the ball, which enables him to remain balanced and give the pass in any direction - and with variable distance and 'weight'. He makes the decisions, so his vision must be excellent as well as his judgement. He must also be able to make a break or to kick - but these are only variations to keep the opposition guessing. He is truly the playmaker.

THE PLAYMAKER

FLY-HALF
special practice

As he must do in a match, the fly-half stands at varying points of distance and depth (A,B,C) relative to his scrum-half, but always putting himself - and the opposition - under pressure. He experiments, trying for breaks or drawing the tackler before off-loading to his centre. A good fly-half can tease the open-side flanker (7), making him run as per the solid, sharply angled line and taking him out of the play - not allowing him to veer out as per the dotted line. In the early 1980s some fascinating battles between the Australian fly-half Mark Ella and the New Zealand flanker Graham Mourie ended with the Australian admitting frustration. He complained that he just couldn't get Mourie to tackle him.

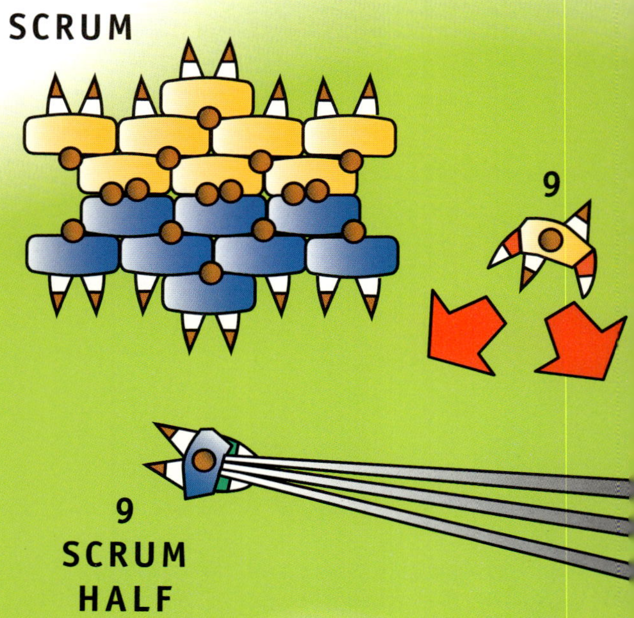

Photo ASP

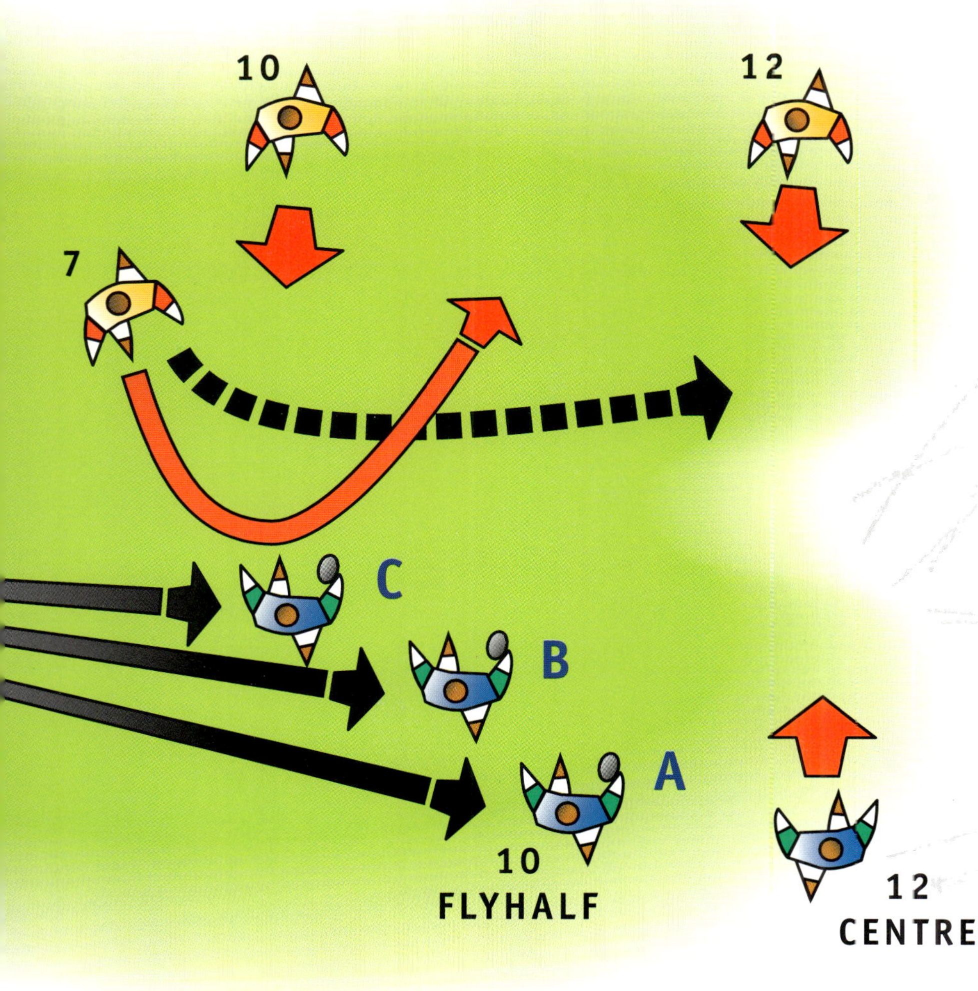
10
12
7
C
B
A
10
FLYHALF
12
CENTRE

Scrum-half

It's confidence that's behind his good pair of hands. And it's his hands which have got him the job, because he's not judged so much on the length of his pass but on the sureness with which he gets his hands on the ball that's often been knocked loose and is bobbling awkwardly. He must not fumble and knock-on; and he must not get caught in possession. The confidence also shows in his enthusiasm for the break, as he exploits his ability, at close quarters, to evade tacklers with subtle body feints and the side-step.

THE CONFIDENCE MAN

He's also an important defender, often covering a great deal of ground to make the final, try-saving tackle. He must kick quickly and well in defence. He must be as tough as old boots, and as agile as a gymnast. A key player, his tenacity and confidence can inspire the side.

WORLD'S BEST

JOOST VAN DER WESTHUIZEN

South Africa

Taller than most scrum halves, and with deceptive strength and speed. Internationally, he made his first big impact with two tries against Scotland in 1994 - the first a stunning, irresistible, break from a scrum 22 metres out. Such breaks have become his trademark.

SCRUM-HALF
special practice

Few, if any, other players ever have to pass the ball off the ground. And since the scrum-half has to do it dozens of times in every game, and under all sorts of pressure, this has to be his special practice. He lays down a row of balls and fires them off, in rapid-fire sequence, to a token fly-half standing some 20 yards away. The receiver shouldn't have to move, should be able to place them all down in another row, allowing the scrum-half to come forward and repeat the routine. With enough practice, the different passes will become second nature.

1. Spin Pass. Starts with rear foot positioned close to ball. Good spread of feet provides solid base and allows ball to be launched without any wind-up. Ball is SWEPT away, the dominant 'near' hand rolling over the ball to provide the spin - which keeps the ball stable in flight.

2. Dive Pass. Usually employed when ball is loose beyond the scrum-half, with forwards breathing down his neck. It gives him an extra half-second, since he can be tackled as he is passing yet still get the ball away. Feet are almost together near to the ball, giving a narrow base from which to pull the ball up and thrust it away. The dive is simply the consequence of a powerful thrust.

SCRUM-HALF

special practice

3. Reverse Pass. Only to be used when facing the wrong way, and with no time to get feet in the desired position. Here, an awkward ball has ballooned from the lineout. From such an upright position the reverse pass requires particular arm strength as well as dexterity and balance. The reverse pass is very much a self-taught skill; only practice will develop it.

❸

adidas
9
adidas

No. 8

Because he locks the scrum, the No. 8 was once thought of as a lock. But he's only a distant relative to the locks who play in the second row. Because he has first touch of the ball in any back row move he must have sure hands, and be able to think on his feet.

WORLD'S BEST

ABDEL BENAZZI

France

The French pack is ever changing, but its centre stone during four Five Nations championships was Benazzi, 6ft 7in and 17 ½ stones, and with pace and handling skills. His mid-field runs penetrate deep and tie in defenders, making him the most dangerous of back row players.

THE BIG CONTROLLER

He must have the close-quarters strength to take the ball forward in the tackle - and, equally, he is a key defender when the opposition are attacking around the side of the scrum. Usually, he is also a lineout jumper. So he has to have the physical presence of a tight forward, plus the pace to roam far and wide with his back row - and a decision-making brain. You could perhaps call him an executive-level tight forward.

No. 8

special practice

To practice defending close to the scrum (or ruck/maul) the No. 8 stands about two paces opposite the attacking player, who has the ball. The latter starts jinking left and right. The defender tracks him, trying to keep directly in the attacker's way. After several seconds of jinking, the attacker tries to drive past the defender. By exchanging roles, attack and defence can be practiced. All back-row forwards will benefit from this drill - and, to varying degrees, so will all forwards and all backs.

NEXT
NEXT

FLANKER

He may be a big man, he may be terrier-sized, but whatever his shape he must be able to run until he drops. In fact, he's likely to be the fittest player in the side, the one whose training most resembles that of the athlete. But as well as being first to the breakdown he also has to do his share of fighting for the ball and, especially, tackling. So he has to be strong, too, in the upper body - especially the arms, since many of his tackles will be just a matter of reaching out with one hand and trying to hold on. So, he has to have the legs and the lungs of a middle-distance track star, and the upper body of a gymnast.

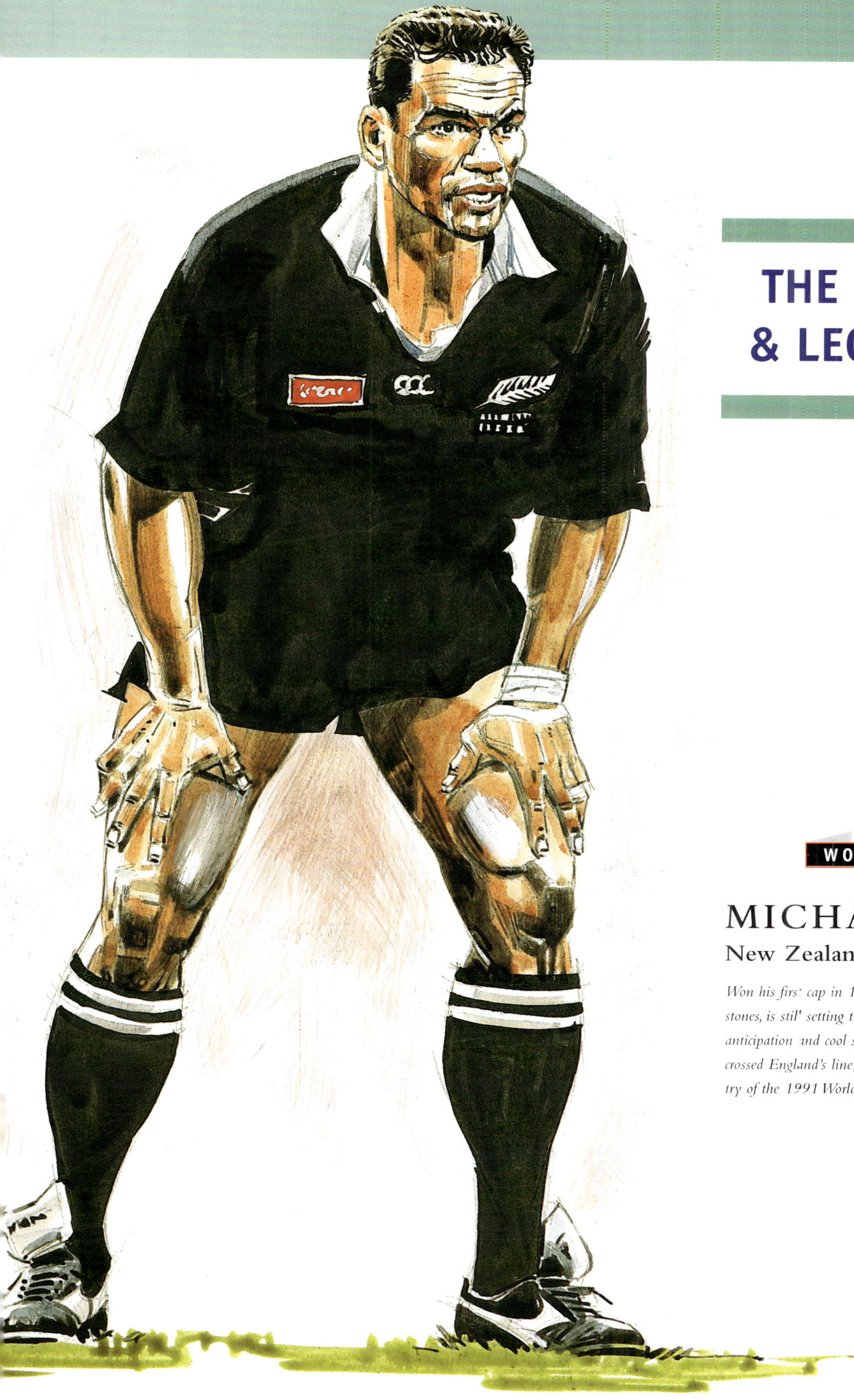

THE LUNGS & LEGS MAN

WORLD'S BEST

MICHAEL JONES

New Zealand

Won his first cap in 1987 and, though a 'mere' 14 ½ stones, is still setting the standard for No. 7s. His speed, anticipation and cool support play was typified when he crossed England's line, clinically and unopposed, for the only try of the 1991 World Cup opener.

FLANKER
special practice

The absolute test for lungs-and-legs is the 'shuttle' or 'beep', test. This involves running backwards and forwards between lines 20 metres apart, the pace dictated by beeps from a timer and quickening every minute until after 17 minutes the intervals are down to 4.36 seconds. Level 17 is the mark reached by the Leicester and England flyer Neil Back - the same as Seb Coe's best! Back can also do 150 press-ups and the same number of sit-ups. His best time for the 30 metres sprint, with a one-step start, is 4.19 seconds.

Photodisc

LOCK

Today's game is not one for huge, lumbering giants at lock. The world's best, like Australia's John Eales and New Zealand's Ian Jones, are tall, strong and quick on their feet. These days you need to be at least 6ft 4in. That means being able to jump and slap your hands against either side of the crossbar - or above it. And just being tall is not enough. The lineout specialist needs 'explosive' strength, like a high-jumper. The type of muscle-fibre he was born with will dictate this to some extent, but it can also be developed by special training. In the scrum, he and his partner are the equivalent of load-bearing walls in a house. It needs a good back, which is flat, straight and locked, and strong legs which straighten to provide the power that will drive the scrum forward. Again, 'explosive' is the word.

THE EXPLOSION EXPERT

You qualify to be an international lock, at least in terms of height, if you can jump and slap your hand against the crossbar (the top edge of which is 3.0 metres from the ground). Slap your hands together *above* the crossbar and you're a worldbeater.

WORLD'S BEST

John Eales
Australia

The man responsible for the amazing lineout dominance of Australia over Wales in their 1991 World Cup match - at half time the lineout 'score' was 17-0 - is now also Captain, and his all round abilities make him, perhaps, the best forward in the world.

LOCK
special practice

Locks need explosive power for lineout jumping - and also, to some extent, for scrummaging. Explosive power involves muscle contractions that are sudden, intense and brief. A series of such contractions, punctuated with short intervals in which the muscle can slacken, is a specific type of training provided by hopping or bounding. But this is exhausting work, so don't overdo it - and don't try it if you're already fatigued.

NEXT
NEXT

PROP

WORLD'S BEST

Jason Leonard

England

He survived a 1992 bone-graft operation on a damaged neck, he switched overnight from loose head to tight head when the 1993 Lions needed him in that position against New Zealand. And in 1996, at 28, the resilient, reliable Jason Leonard became England's most capped prop.

The prop is one of the few players who has the chance regularly to embarrass his opponent, and enjoy it. But there's only one possible physique that will allow him to play there; a short stature, and the neck, shoulders and chest of a weight-lifter. Whether he will play loose-head or tight-head, though, is another matter, and can only be decided by playing in each position. In some ways, loose-head is the more difficult role, for his head is outside his opponent's, and he has to stop being split away. By contrast, the tight-head can enjoy doing just that, within the limits of the laws - though he also bears the brunt of the pressure generated by two sets of eight forwards. Thus, the tight-head may be a little shorter. But both props must be mentally tough and enjoy confrontation. And both know that above all they must keep their scrum steady and solid on their own put-in. It is a tricky balance, between stability and aggression.

THE ROCK

PROP

special practice

Like rutting stags, two players engage as if in a one-against-one scrum and try to force each other back from the line beneath them. But this widely-used drill is much more than a shoulder-strengthening exercise. One coach calls it 'Hit and Stick', for the main object is stability - avoiding an all-too-easy collapse into the ground. Bent knees mean it's easier to keep the back horizontal and maintain a good attitude of shoulders and head, and thus stay balanced. And so the two opponents 'stick'. This may be a prime exercise for props, but all other scrummagers will benefit - and, indeed, all rugby players.

HOOKER

MOBILITY MAN

Hookers are supreme competitors. Often they have come to the position having started elsewhere (perhaps as a scrum-half or flanker) simply because they've spotted an opportunity. That's in their nature - seizing chances. It also explains why they tend to come in a greater variety of shapes than props, though they certainly have to be strong enough to hold a position and also be fairly flexible. A tough man, the hooker shares his front row's desire to

conquer the opposition, yet his position at the front of the lineout also makes him a kind of flanker, foraging in the open spaces and handling at speed. Add to all this the need for precise throwing-in at the lineout, and the hooker becomes a rather fascinating mix of abilities and temperament. But there's no doubt that being at the heart of the scrum makes him a natural leader. Like the scrum-half, his attitude can inspire the side.

WORLD'S BEST

Sean Fitzpatrick

New Zealand

The world's most capped hooker, the best thrower in to the lineout, and like all hookers ferociously competitive. Grew into the captaincy wl.en given it in 1992, thrived on the new incentive, and in 1996 became the first All Black captain to win a series in South Africa.

HOOKER
special practice

With a support for his right shoulder (eg: a goal-post) a hooker can practice his speed of strike. As much as anything this is speed of reaction, and the practice also works well when an object like an orange or coin is dropped, as if into a scrum, and from varying heights. The ball, however, is necessary when the hooker wants to practice deflecting it on different angles, or 'channels'.

Photo Andrew Maw

How gifts of ambition, strength and confidence were brought to Rugby Union

The Northern Stars

Rugby Union suddenly became a new game as the 1996-97 season exploded into action in England. The cause was partly new laws, and agreement between referees, coaches and players as to how they should be applied. There was also a new desire by professional players to raise their standards. And the third factor was the influence of the Rugby League players at, especially, Bath, Harlequins and Wasps.

The dazzling skills of Jason Robinson and Henry Paul had already shaken Rugby Union men in the dual code games between Wigan and Bath. Now, the darting feet and the upper body strength of such players started to spell out some important messages ...

1. Run the ball back at your opponents. It is much more effective than kicking it back and handing over possession.

2. Have a go at beating the man who stands in your way. If he should stop you, trust in your strength to at least hold him off until help arrives.

Gary Connolly

(Wigan, Harlequins, England and Great Britain)

Not the most outwardly or most obviously gifted of players, less "flashy" than most, hardly the quickest either. What makes him stand out is that he does the basics so well. His tackling is ferocious and fearless and he is one of the best around at timing the pass. Like all League players he is strong in the upper body. Despite suffering from Pneumonia at the start of the (three week) 1995 World Cup, he recovered to play a full 80 minutes in the final. A direct runner.

In one match, when Robinson played at fullback, Bath Coach Brian Ashton, bet him that in this position he would have to kick at some point in the match. Ashton lost the bet. Robinson never kicked, not once.

At another game, TV cameras gave viewers a new insight into how defenders might be taken on. Here, at Harlequins, Robbie Paul seemed to be blocked by several defenders. He ran at one, turned his back, shaped to pass, then spun out of the tackle and half circled around to do exactly the same to another defender.

In the same game, the pace and strength of Gary Connolly consistently took him several yards past his opponent. The typical Rugby Union centre would be unlikely to try that, unless he saw a gap. He would be worried that he would be tackled without support, thus he looks to unload while still able to. No doubt the confidence of the Rugby League men stemmed from the fact that in their own code they're not embarrassed to be taken to the ground: they can always hold on to the ball, then get up and play it. However,

Henry Paul

(Wigan, Bath and New Zealand)

Probably the most naturally gifted rugby footballer in Britain. What sets him apart from the rest is his quick feet and balance. He can run around opponents but seems to enjoy side stepping / jinking past them more. He often "shows" the ball when doing that. At his best, especially in open play, when he runs slightly across the field and then cuts back in between defenders.

Robbie Paul

(Bradford Bulls and Harlequins)

Made his mark at the Headquarters of Rugby Union when, in the Middlesex Sevens, he produced a side step that sent most of the crowd the wrong way. An even better one illuminated the Challenge Cup Final where he seemed not only to wrong foot the defence, but increase his pace off the right foot, when mortals have to slow down by dint of planting a boot down so firmly. Like his brother, a lovely runner but better over shorter distances. The famous rugby league coach, Alex Murphy, always said that the way to score tries was to keep the ball alive for as long as possible. That's what the Pauls try to do.

there was no question that they had developed the strength and the appetite to take opponents on - often with the aid of the strong hand off so common in the League code.

Photo Andrew Maw

A Union back with the ball tends to be thinking about the next ruck or maul. "We've tended to neglect the idea of going one against one," admits Bob Dwyer, ex Coach of the World Champion Wallabies. "In League, by comparison, questions are posed of defensive players every few seconds."

Dwyer isn't a huge fan of Rugby League: he says it involves "a small number of highly developed skills". But he likes the way players in every position have to run fast, and he would particularly like to see the mental attitude of League brought into Union. "In League they're mentally aggressive, self starting. There's a feeling of 'let me at 'em'. Give a League player the ball and he immediately initiates an attack. Whereas the Union player often seems to be thinking, 'I wonder if I'm going left or right'."

Va'aiga Tuigamala

(Wigan, Newcastle and Western Samoa)

When introduced to League he was a joke and looked like a candidate for the worst buy ever. Since then, with early heavy emphasis on fitness - moving the weight from his backside to his chest - he emerged to reveal skills that were never dreamed of when he was just a battering ram for the All Blacks. Still fearsome on the hoof, he's learnt how to unload the ball from unlikely positions and with surprising dexterity. A prime example of his craft was the League match against Bath where, despite having three men on him, and the ball seemingly tucked under his arm, it popped out from a mass of bodies to a team mate. Such skill has turned him into a centre, rather than a winger.

Jason Robinson

(Wigan, Bath, England and Great Britain)

He always looks as though he's making ground when he runs, even if he actually doesn't. Turned into a winger because he would never get a game at scrum-half, he has quick feet which he keeps moving, giving the impression of advancement. As a runner his prime weapon is the jink - often at 180 degrees. A pure, instinctive runner, always looking for gaps. An active looking runner rather than the languid Henry Paul or the powerful Connolly. With blinding insight for which sportsmen are renowned, his nickname is "Billy Whizz".

Down at Bath, Ashton was particularly impressed by what the instinctive, jack-in-the-box running of Robinson meant in TACTICAL terms. "He doesn't hit the line in the conventional sense, and he is very quick off the mark, so he creates space in a totally different way". It meant, he said, that Bath could just let Robinson do his thing, rather than call moves. " Defences are organised to defend against predictable moves. So defending against this sort of ability can be quite difficult."

By the mid season, as most of the League men prepared to return North, it was being said that their influence had begun to wane. Perhaps the truth was that the gap had begun to close because their example had been followed. They may simply have inspired team mates and opponents to new levels of skill and ambition.

NEXT
NEXT

Skills & Techniques

The Kicks

PUNT (*Screw Kick*)

If it's spinning, the ball is more stable through the air and goes further. The ball is held on an angle across the line of the boot, which strikes through the centre of the ball. A hand on top of the ball will place it more accurately on the boot and give a tighter spin, therefore more length. Kickers are taught to have an image in their minds of placing the ball in the air, as it were. 'Putting it on the shelf' is one popular term. So is the instruction to kick the ball 'through the gate' (an imaginary gate between the hands). The focus is thus on the quality of the strike rather than on the intended destination of the ball.

DROP KICK

Unlike the Punt, it usually requires the momentum of at least a couple of steps as shown above. The last step is a long one, as the ball is dropped almost vertically but tilted very slightly backwards. It lands only inches in front of the non-kicking foot and rebounds fractionally before impact. The fault of lifting the head can afflict the drop kick even more than other kicks, so make sure to keep watching the ball right through the impact.

GOAL KICK

These days the ball is generally placed upright, or even tilting very slightly forwards. 'Addressing' the ball, the kicker places his kicking foot directly behind it and his other foot at hips width distance to the side. This is the point to which that foot must return after he has retreated and then run in, as shown below. Getting this right is critical, for the non kicking foot being too far to right or left is the biggest reason for a kick missing. *Continued over.*

③

②

③

②

1

GOAL KICK *continued*

The run is usually on a slight curve, with the foot almost at right angles to the ball at impact. Imagine a tennis ball at the centre of the rugby ball, and the middle of the instep bone driving straight through to it. After contact, the leg swings across the line of the kick, but this should only happen as a natural part of the follow through. It shouldn't be happening as the kick is made, when the focus should be on kicking THROUGH the ball and AT the posts.

Most top kickers have experimented with various styles, and some have experimented by stripping their technique right back to the basics. This has meant striking the ball from a standing position - just getting used to swinging the kicking leg and the feel of good contact, never mind how far the ball goes so long as it is going straight. Imagine, too, that you are driving the knee at the ball - like a golfer thinking about hitting with his wrists.

1

THE TACKLE

Straight On

The most important component in any tackle is the drive of the shoulder into the body, generated by the tackler's leg power. Here, the drive is so powerful that the ball carrier is lifted off his feet and falls backwards. The tackler's arms simply follow on from the drive, but a tackle made just with the arms will be no match for the force of the ball carrier's legs. Note the head to one side of the hips, a key requirement in any tackle.

From the Side

In our demonstration, the tackler has chased a scrum-half who has run wide from a scrum, and launched himself with full commitment to make a perfect tackle. If the tackler can get both feet off the ground he will make his weight count to greater effect, and become a missile that is almost certain to 'down' the opponent.

1

2

From Behind

Ideally, the impact area is initially the small of the back or waist, with the arms then sliding down to 'lasso' the ball carrier around the thighs. Depending on the relative speeds and strengths of the players, it may be possible for the tackler to take one hand down to seize an ankle, or take it up to grab an arm and shake the ball loose.

THE SCRUMMAGE

2

A scrum starts with the hooker standing upright, hands up by his head. He binds over the shoulders of his props, gripping tightly on their shirts, while they use their inside arms to grip him around the waist. The three thus start with a platform which is intended to stay intact come what may - and which will transmit the power which is going to come from behind.

The two locks link by gripping each other around the waist. To join the front row they force their weight up until their heads are between the thighs of prop and hooker - which shouldn't be easy, if the front row is tightly bound - and then force their heads up until their outside shoulder is hitting against the junction of thigh and buttock. Their drive is ready to be transmitted up each prop's spine. They may rest on either knee until the two packs engage.

Each flanker joins at a slight angle, though his inside shoulder will be square enough to supply extra drive through the outside of the prop's thigh / buttock.

The No. 8 forces his head between the two locks, gripping them around their hips. He keeps his head up and his feet well back and wide apart.

Photo Andrew Maw

Front row and locks may try different foot positioning but all eight forwards must observe the cardinal rule of scrummaging: backs straight and heads up. Even top class sides sometimes forget this rule, as they become distracted by the intensity of the battle. The other element is tight binding. Just tightening the grip can drive the scrum forward.

4

THE LINEOUT

The hooker holds the ball, near the rear end, in both hands before bringing it back in one hand, elbow bent, and launching it torpedo style.

The elbow's transition from back movement to forward movement is the trigger for the jumper at No. 2 to start his leap - so this timing, plus the right height and weight, means that the throw is perhaps the most important element in a successful lineout.

❷

The prop at the front of the lineout has already started to support the jumper. Under the law, this can only be done after the jumper is airborne and the supporting hands must be no lower than waist level.

❸

❹

❺

Supported also from behind, the jumper makes a two handed catch and brings the ball down to his chest, turning as he does so to ensure that he lands with good, protected possession.

THE MAUL

Typically, the maul has been created from controlled lineout possession, or as a result of a player being tackled and staying on his feet. The side in possession has a wall of players, tightly bound, who have been able to resist any interference from the opposition and comfortably smuggle the ball back hand to hand. Here, the final recipient hands the ball between his legs to give his scrum half silver plate possession.

THE RUCK

Rucks have also been called loose scrums, since the players are bound together in a rough scrummage fashion - and (unlike a maul) the ball is on the ground. Here, and overleaf, the players are well bound and have adopted good scrummaging positions as they practice driving over the man on the ground. *Continued over.*

But to achieve this isn't easy. It's a matter of making order out of the chaos which generally exists in the aftermath of a tackle and disputed possession. It is all too easy for players to fall down and add to the wreckage - or, in trying not to, to adopt very upright positions, as in mauling. But the ruck challenges players to use their strength and technique to stay on their feet, and to try and adopt low, scrummaging positions.

The All Blacks have always been regarded as the rucking experts. They make a point of getting low, and even start to bind together, as they come in their twos and threes to 'hit' a ruck.

2

3

4

5

HANDLING

These days, the emphasis is increasingly on ALL players sharpening their handling skills. Players are realising, too, that these 'skills' aren't necessarily acts of wizardry that are beyond mere mortals. Often it's a matter of little more than confidence. As Bob Dwyer says to players: "Don't blame the bad pass for dropping the ball. If you can get your hand to the ball you should be able to catch it. You can do it if you believe it." Here are just four of the many practice routines that can help players to put faith in their hands and their reflexes ...

1. Concentric Circles

Players form a large circle with red and yellow jerseys alternating. Starting at the same point, the Yellows pass the ball clockwise, the Reds anti-clockwise. It's a race, testing not only speed of pass but also control and accuracy - since each passer has to ignore the 'opposition' jersey that is almost in the line of his pass. This exercise encourages hands-only passes and minimum body movement - which players are encouraged to translate into their passing as they run up and down the field. Once, a swing of the hips (and slight pause) was thought to be helpful in a pass. Now, players are told: "Run with your legs, pass with your hands".

2. Pairs

In this reaction exercise, which mimics a ball bouncing loose among forwards, two players standing a metre apart have a ball lobbed between them at about shoulder height. The first player to get his hands on the ball also has to protect what he has won by whipping the ball out of his opponent's reach and turning his back.

3. Ball on Back

Player's knees are flexed and body angled slightly so that the ball will roll quickly, rather than fall, when the helper lets go. When the player feels the ball moving he has to clap his hands and then reach behind him to catch the ball.

4. Fast Hands

Crouching, the player holds ball beneath buttocks. Letting go, he has to clap his hands in front of him and then catch it before it hits the ground. Alternatively, player holds ball between legs, one hand from the front and the other from the rear. He has to reverse the hands without the ball hitting the ground.

4

DIET & FITNESS

FITNESS

The theory of training holds good for all types of physical training: the body responds to work and begins to adapt to it, thus becoming more efficient. Thus, it can handle a bigger 'workload' or it can handle the same workload more easily.

Work comes in many forms on a rugby field, and all players need - in different degrees - the Three Big S's:

SPEED, STRENGTH, STAMINA

Obviously, the emphasis varies greatly between backs and forwards. And the variation between certain forwards clearly varies as much - for example, between prop and flanker. None the less, the players who depend greatly on speed cannot afford to ignore strength and power. Equally, the strong men must also do as much speed work as possible. Remember: while every player should develop his strengths to the maximum, his game is likely to show the most dramatic improvement through work on its weaker areas. The following advice, therefore, applies not only to those identified but, perhaps in moderation, to all players ...

SPEED WORK (wings, fullback, centres). 'Intervals' of 6 x 50 metres. Use a 'rolling' start, then the full 50m. Jog slowly back between each, taking at least a minute. Aim for top speed but try to do it comfortably, without straining. In time, sprinting will seem easier, more fluid, but improvements in PURE speed require you to focus on leg action. Concentrate in some runs on maximum (but comfortable) length of stride, in others on leg-speed. In runs over 100 metres, try 20-30 seconds of each. Then try sprinting with a high knee lift. Mixing up these varying elements ought eventually to produce greater speed with a 'natural' action.

STRENGTH (props, hooker, locks) Pure strength training is not to be recommended to young players, whose bones and bodies are still growing. Top-level props, for example, are half-way to being weight lifters with the maximum-weight 'dead lifts' and bench presses. Much better for young players, and players in all positions, are lifts using bar bells or dumb bells (eg: 'curling' the weight from waist to neck) in 'sets' of ten. Select a weight with which the eighth, ninth and tenth lifts need considerable effort. After a one minute rest, another set, and three sets in all.

It may be accurate to describe such training in terms of POWER rather than STRENGTH. Power is the product of speed and strength, and allows explosive action - which is needed for most rugby action.

STAMINA (all forwards, especially back row). Stamina may also be called endurance. It allows the player to maintain his speed around the field for 80 minutes. Long, 'aerobic' runs (30-60 minutes) enable you generally to 'keep up with the play' and see the game out. Shorter 'interval' work helps you keep going in short, hard bursts without getting exhausted. Although the length of a typical burst may be only 30-40 metres, the training needed to adapt the body's oxygen supply system to such demand requires that the distances are rather longer - 200 to 400 metres. Each run should be at three-quarter effort (eg: if your flat out speed for 300 metres is 45 seconds, in about 55 seconds). The rest between each should be 2-3 minutes. When you can handle, say, six such runs, look for improvement by increasing the number of runs, or the speed, or shorten the interval - or a combination of all three.

Another very challenging (but rewarding) routine involves marking a 400 metre track into 50 metre sections. Each sprint (semi fast) will be of just 50 metres, followed by slow jog recovery, but you don't stop. Experiment to work out a pattern you can maintain for, say, two or three laps. The sprint section might be followed by two recovery sections (100 metres) or even by three. When you've established a pattern you can maintain, follow it for up to three miles (12 laps). Then, in time, vary the pattern. Perhaps alternate the recovery sections between three sections and two, then between two and one. If you can end up shortening each recovery phase to one section (ie: 50 metres sprint and 50 metres recovery), and you can maintain it for the full distance, you will have become an international athlete!

DIET

Beer and big steaks are definitely out of fashion. Go into a professional side's clubhouse around the time of morning training and you will see just what a modern sporting breakfast is based on: mountains of sliced bread and cartons of fruit juice.

As for the 'traditional' steak, it's likely to put on unnecessary weight - and it will take upwards of 24 hours to digest. The emphasis these days is on carbohydrates to supply energy, lots of fluid, and plenty of snacks - rather than a small number of big meals.

NOTE: The fourth 'S' is Suppleness, and all the above training - especially the speed work - should be preceded by warm up exercises. It is particularly important to stretch calf and hamstring muscles, also hip, back and arms. Above all, make sure the body has become WARM. That means you're perspiring.

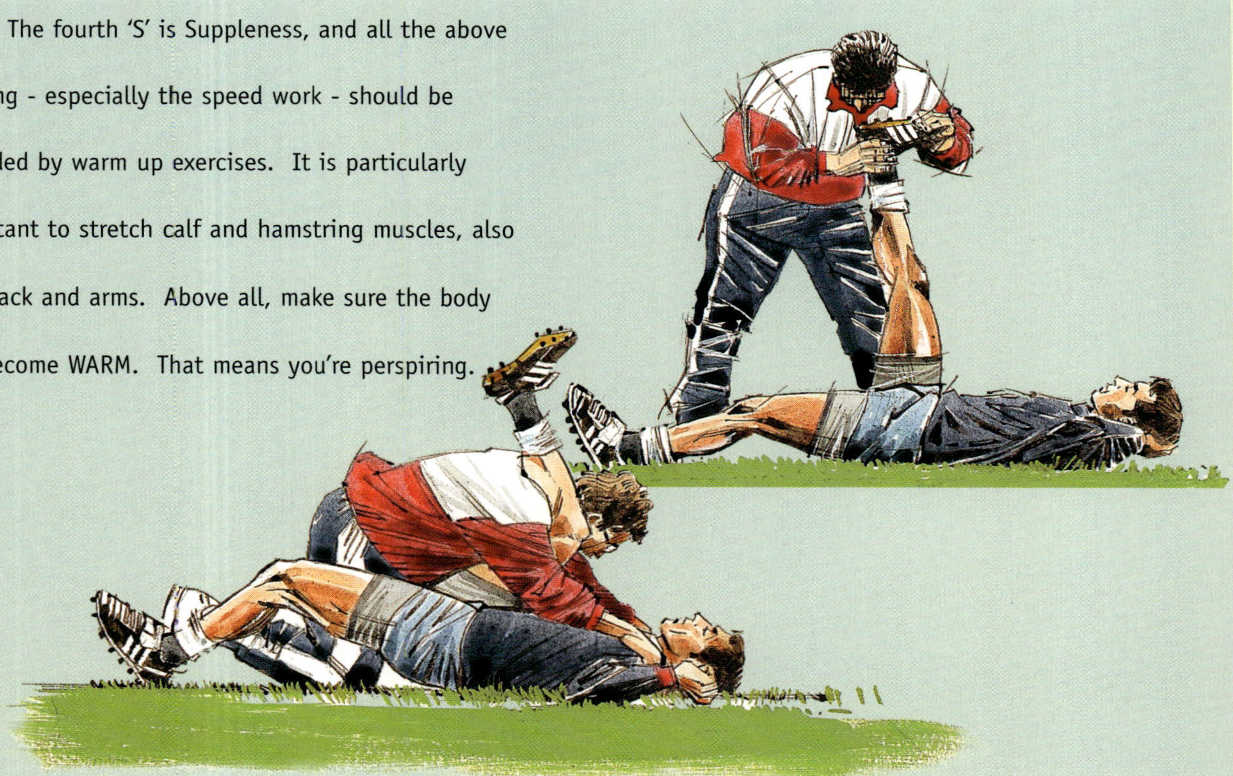

Energy is stored within the muscles as glycogen, and intensive or prolonged exercise will deplete it. So keep fuelling up. The following foods (taken as a snack or small meal) will supply you with carbohydrate:

Bread, potatoes, pasta and rice.

Fruit and vegetables.

Breakfast cereals and porridge. Either could also be used as a late evening snack.

Baked beans on toast.

Ice cream and milk shakes.

Branded cereal bars (eg: Jordans and Tracker).

Also:

Eat lean white meat (eg: chicken and turkey) or fish rather than red meat.

Avoid cooking fat and oil. Grill rather than fry.

Drink even when you're not feeling thirsty: at least two glasses of fluid with each meal or snack (fruit juice diluted 50-50 with water) plus sports drinks like Isotar or Gatorade.

Variety will give you a better result than eating the same each day.

MENTAL TRAINING

These days, before a match, spectators tend not to hear concerted shouting and the thunder of studs on dressing room floors. 'Geeing up' is largely discredited, for players want to be in control in the hectic, tense, opening minutes, not OUT of control.

More likely, the hooker is visualising his first throw into the lineout, the fullback the foot placement, swing, and the impact in his first kick at goal. Players may even be silently reciting some personal 'mantras'. And there will be personal stereos in play.

It is, however, still possible that certain players will need to motivate themselves and become more aggressive. Others may just want to feel inspired. Some will seek to be calm. Each to his own, then. Choose your own music, or your own recorded words. All it needs is an honest assessment of your own needs.

If there is a problem area in your game - and most players do have some weaknesses - the chances are that you worry about it too much. It might, for example, be a fear of the front-on tackle. The classic remedy is to ask yourself what your main strength is - for example, having lots of stamina. So you try to over-ride your fearful, negative thoughts with your most positive ones. Taking the above examples, this might mean that you keep saying to yourself: "I can run and run, and I will out-run anyone in this game".

Another player may have a mantra in which he repeats: "I am calm and focused and always have time". And yet another's may be: "I am a mad dog, and nobody enjoys playing against me". Again, each to his own!

COPING WITH INJURY

(An article kindly supplied by Vulkan UK Ltd)

With the increasing demands of the modern game on the body, players have had to become stronger, faster, fitter and more competitive. Remaining injury free using the correct management and treatment of injuries is now an important part of the game and is vital in ensuring that players are back to fitness as quickly as possible.

It is important to warm up fully and stretch each body part prior to training or competitive games. A warmed up muscle or joint is better able to cope with an injury and their injury will be less severe. Warming down and stretching off after exercise is equally important, as it helps to avoid stiffness and muscle soreness after.

If an injury does occur, then always take the advice of the club physio/doctor, as the correct assessment and treatment in the early phase of an injury can make a dramatic difference to the recovery time. Always follow the R.I.C.E. procedure for the first 36-48 hours, where the injured muscle, joint or limb is Rested, Ice is applied frequently for up to 20 minutes at a time to reduce the pain, a Compression bandage is used to reduce the swelling and the injured area should be Elevated to reduce the bloodflow. During this phase, heat, such as hot baths should be avoided. Heat may be applied after 48 hours, once the swelling has subsided.

The injury area will then gradually become stronger through the body's natural healing process and by introducing remedial exercises to strengthen the injured area. Up to and following recovery, the area should always be stretched to increase the range of movement and complete the recovery process.

The Vulkan neoprene thermal supports play an important part in the prevention and treatment of injuries. They work by insulating the body's heat and so help prevent injuries from occurring by maintaining higher tissue temperature during exercise, they provide support to the injured muscle or joint, increase the bloodflow and increase the oxygen to the injured area, so helping to speed up the body's natural healing process. They cushion against knocks and blows and help improve the confidence of the player during training or playing.

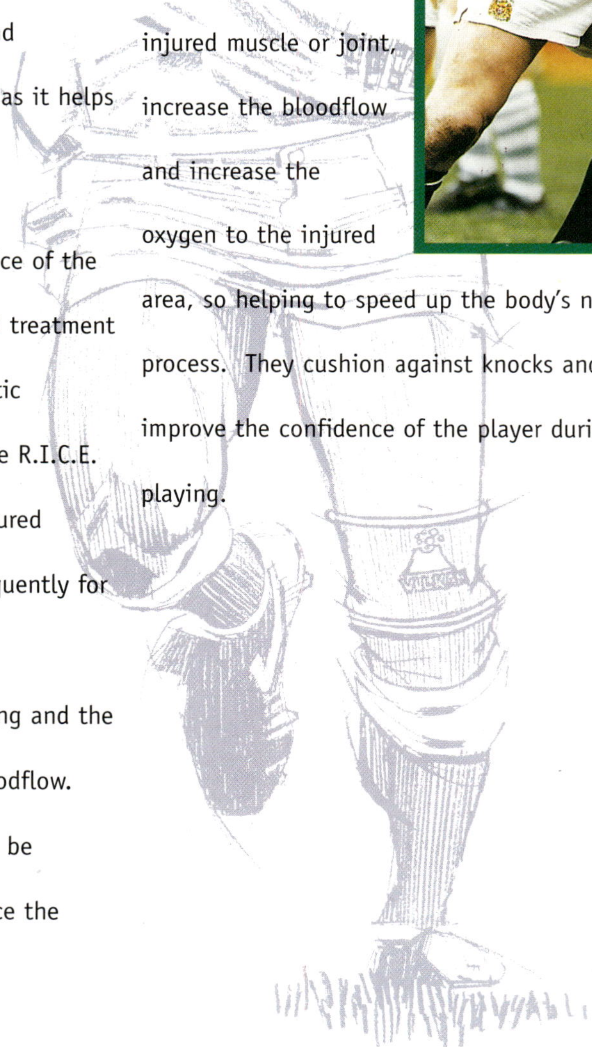